W9-AYE-655

Let's Investigate Marvelously Meaningful Maps

Madelyn Wood Carlisle

Illustrations by Yvette Santiago Banek

BARRON'S

© Copyright 1992 by Barron's Educational Series, Inc.

All rights reserved.
No part of this book may be reproduced in any form by photostat,
microfilm, xerography, or any other means, or incorporated into
any information retrieval system, electronic or mechanical,
without the written permission of the copyright owner.

All inquiries should be addressed to:
Barron's Educational Series, Inc.
250 Wireless Boulevard
Hauppauge, NY 11788

International Standard Book No. 0-8120-4735-4

Library of Congress Catalog Card No. 92-19788

Library of Congress Cataloging-in Publication Data

Carlisle, Madelyn Wood.
    Let's investigate marvelously meaningful maps / by Madelyn Wood Carlisle;
illustrations by Yvette Santiago Banek.
        p.   cm.
    Includes index.
    Summary: Introduces all kinds of maps including weather, topographic, road,
and undersea; and explains such terms as scale, projections, symbols, latitude,
and longitude.
    ISBN 0-8120-4735-4
    1. Maps—Juvenile literature.   [1. Maps.]   I. Title.
GA130.C27   1992
912—dc20   92-19788
                                                                    CIP
                                                                    AC

PRINTED IN HONG KONG
2345 9927 98765432

Contents

All Kinds of Maps

Pirates of long ago often buried their loot. Many failed to get back to dig it up again.

Wouldn't you like to find an old map that showed you where a pirate treasure had been buried?

X marks the spot!

Wouldn't it be exciting to find an old map that showed you how to find a buried treasure?

The pirates who once roamed the seas, boarding other ships and stealing their cargoes, often had to hide their loot in a hurry. The beaches of Central America and the United States, and the islands off the coasts, were some of their favorite hiding places.

Chests filled with gold, silver, and jewels may still lie buried in the sands.

Even if you are never so lucky as to find a map that will lead you to a long-lost treasure, there are many wonderful things you can find out from other kinds of maps.

Maps show us how to get from one place to another, but they do a lot more than that. They can tell us about the kinds of people who live in different places. They can show us what crops are grown where, and where there are mountains, rivers, and lakes. They tell us about forests, and rainfall, and tomorrow's weather. By looking at a map we can see where we can go camping, what historic places we can visit, where railroads run, and where there are mines, pipelines, caves, and castles.

Maps show us our location on planet Earth, and just where we are in our country, our state, our city or town—even our own block.

People have been making maps for thousands of years. The first drawing that any human being ever made may have been a map sketched with a stick in the dirt. Maps became important to people who traveled long distances to trade with other tribes. When people began to build boats and sail the seas, they drew maps of the coastlines they discovered so that the sailors who followed them would find their way safely.

We make maps of more than just our own planet Earth. We make sky maps that show the constellations of stars at different times of the year. We have mapped the surface of the moon. Satellites sent out into space even help us make maps of other planets.

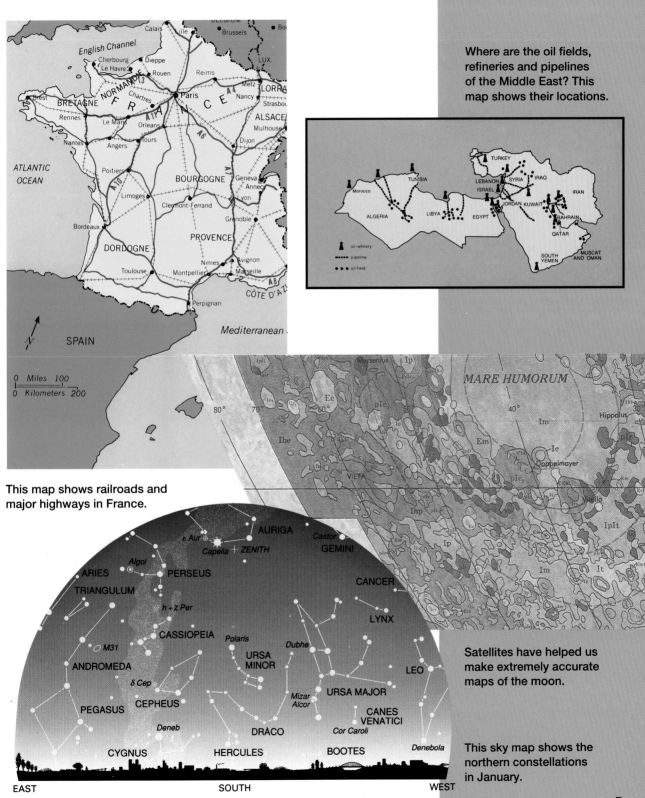

Where are the oil fields, refineries and pipelines of the Middle East? This map shows their locations.

This map shows railroads and major highways in France.

Satellites have helped us make extremely accurate maps of the moon.

This sky map shows the northern constellations in January.

If You Make a Map

Have you ever made a map? Maybe you thought up an imaginary place and drew a picture of it.

Or have you made what we call a relief map? That's a map in three dimensions, which you mold instead of draw. Hills and mountains rise up on the surface of a relief map.

It's a lot of fun to dream up a new world. You can make the continents on it any shape you want them to be. You can decide which one you would like to live on and draw a city or town there. Or a big farm or ranch. If you want a lake by your land you can just put one there. You can make whole mountain ranges.

Maybe you will make a map of a make-believe world that you want to keep for yourself alone, but most maps are for showing and sharing.

Did you ever write to someone and send a map to show how you walk to school? You might have made squares for all the blocks and then drawn a dotted line from your house to your school. Your map might have shown that you turn right at the third corner and then walk two more blocks.

Modeling clay or newspapers soaked in a mixture of flour and water are good materials for making relief maps.

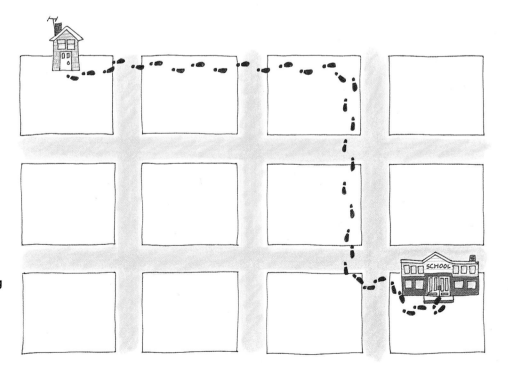

Maps show an area as if you were looking down on it from a very tall building or an airplane. If you walk to school, a map showing your path from door to door might look something like this.

Or maybe you moved to a different house and wanted to show a friend what your new home was like. You drew what is called a floor plan, showing all the rooms. Maybe you made a floor plan of just your own room. A floor plan is a kind of map.

If you are making a map to tell something to somebody else, you have to make your map easy to understand. Let's say you want to make a map of the block or road you live on, showing how many dogs and cats live in each house and how many trees there are on your street.

If you draw a dog for every dog, a cat for every cat, and a tree for every tree, you would not have to explain what your map was telling. But it's a lot faster and simpler to choose marks that stand for dogs, cats, and trees. Such marks are called symbols.

Suppose the symbol you choose for a dog is a red circle, for a cat a blue square, and for a tree a green triangle. You know what those marks stand for but you have to make what is called a "legend" for your map if you want other people to know too.

This is what your map and its legend might look like:

If you use symbols on a map to show the number of dogs, cats, and trees on your block, your map's legend must explain what each symbol means.

MARVELOUS MAPS IN THREE DIMENSIONS

Relief maps give a three-dimensional view of an area and are fun to look at. They are more than fun for blind people, who can use their fingers to "see" the shapes of a certain location, such as the place where they live. A relief map of Boston has the buildings and curbings raised, and the streets and sidewalks textured. A blind peson can explore the city by feel and can learn how to get from one place to another.

The largest map ever made is a relief map. It is a scale model of the whole state of California, with all its mountain ranges, hills, valleys, towns, and cities. It is 450 feet (137 meters) long and weighs 86,000 pounds (39,000 kilograms). It is so big and heavy that a good place to display it has yet to be found.

There's a relief map that's not that big but that shows a whole country. If you ever go to Guatemala City, you can walk around this large three-dimensional map of Guatemala. It's in an outdoor park and is made of concrete so it can't be damaged by the weather. The features on the map are maked with little flags so you can learn the names of the mountains, rivers, and towns in that Central American country.

A Scale for Your Map

One of the most important things the legend on a map tells is what scale was used in drawing the map. By scale we mean how much space on the map stands for how much space on the ground or in your house or your room.

If you want your map to be accurate, you have to choose what scale you will use. We say maps are drawn "to scale," or, if they are just roughly sketched, "not to scale."

If you are drawing a map of your room you will choose a different scale from the one you would use if you were going to make a map of the United States or one showing how you walk to school.

For the map of your room you might decide that 1 inch on your map will stand for 1 foot in your room. If your room measures 10 feet by 11 feet, your map will be 10 inches by 11 inches.

But the United States is 3,000 miles wide. To draw a map of the United States to the scale of 1 inch equals 1 mile, you would have to have a piece of paper 3,000 inches long!

If you want your map of the United States to fit on a sheet of paper 10 inches wide, 1 inch on your paper will have to stand for 300 miles.

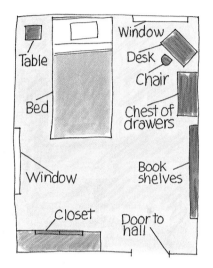

This room map (or floor plan) measures 2 inches by 2$\frac{1}{2}$ inches. The room it represents is actually 8 feet by 10 feet. So the scale for this map is $\frac{1}{4}$ inch = 1 foot.

The size of the paper you must have for a map of the United States depends on the scale you use.

If you have an Atlas in your home, look at the maps for different countries. You will see that many different scales were used. That's because the countries are different sizes, and yet the makers of the Atlas want each large country, or grouping of smaller countries, to fit on a page of the same size.

It's easy for you to see that if you want Korea and Japan (the island nation that is west of Korea) to fit on a page that's the same size as the page with the map of China on it, then they will have to be drawn to different scales.

The scale you choose for a map you make will depend on how big you want your finished map to be, or what size sheet of paper it has to fit onto.

On this map, Korea and Japan are shown in red.

CHINA

The scale of this map of China is 1 inch = 500 miles. If a map of Japan and Korea (top) were to occupy a space of the same size, the scale would be 1 inch = 200 miles.

The Map that Named America

You probably know that both North and South America are named for Amerigo Vespucci. Vespucci was an Italian who sailed across the Atlantic Ocean to what is now South America in 1499 and again in 1501. He explored many miles of the coastline.

Since Vespucci's voyages were made later than those of Christopher Columbus, why aren't the Americas named for Columbus instead of Vespucci? One reason may be that Columbus never did believe that he had come to a place that the people of Europe had never known was there. Vespucci was sure he had come to a new world. Of course, to the people who lived there it wasn't a new world at all. Their ancestors had lived on both of the continents for centuries.

It wasn't Vespucci who gave his name to the land he visited. He said it should be called Mundus Novus, which is Latin for New World. He wrote letters and reports about his discoveries. He described the natives and told about the way they lived.

A German mapmaker named Martin Waldseemuller was fascinated by these stories. He thought the newly discovered lands should be named after Vespucci. By then Vespucci had changed his first name from Amerigo

Amerigo Vespucci, the man for whom the continents of North and South America are named.

This famous illustration shows Christopher Columbus and his crew landing in the New World.

to Americus. For a book published in 1507, Waldseemuller put this new world on a map and printed on it a new name: America.

Columbus had sailed from Spain, so the Spanish didn't like that choice of a name. For three hundred years they called the newly discovered lands Columbia. But the name America was the one that stuck. Why did Vespucci change his name from Amerigo to Americus? Most people thought that he just wanted to use the Latin form of his name. But one historian gave a different reason. He said that Vespucci changed his name to Americus after he came to know some New World natives who called themselves "Amerrique." In their language the name meant "a spirit that breathes life itself."

Don't you like to think that that's the real meaning of the name America?

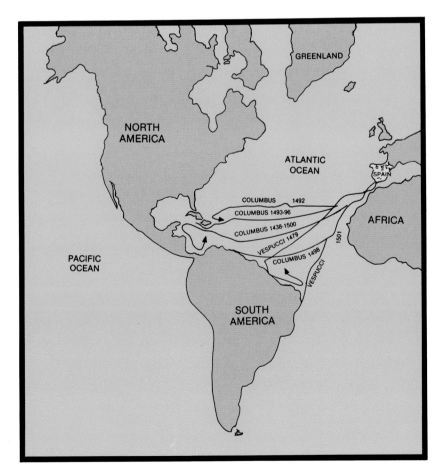

Every voyage of the early explorers gave mapmakers new knowledge of our world.

HISTORIC AMERICAN MAPS

The Map that Fooled Columbus.
Columbus may have discovered America because of an incorrect map drawn by Paolo Toscanelli, an Italian mapmaker. Toscanelli's map showed India as being only a couple of thousand miles (about 3,000 kilometers) west of Europe. Columbus figured he could sail his ships that far and so he set out across the Atlantic Ocean. As you know, the land he came to was not India but what was later to become America.

The First Map of an American City.
The oldest known map of an American city shows St. Augustine, Florida. It was drawn in 1588, more than 400 years ago.

The First Map Printed in America.
The first map printed in America was offered for sale in 1783. It showed what was then known about the geography of the United States. The land that now makes up the western states was not drawn on this map because that part of the country was almost completely unknown at the time.

The First Automobile Road Map.
If your family travels by automobile, you have probably looked at road maps to find the best way to go. The first map in America made especially for motorists was printed in 1914 and showed only the roads around Pittsburgh.

Round World on a Flat Map

Look at this map of the world. Compare the sizes of Africa and Greenland. They seem to be about the same, don't they? But Africa is really many times larger than Greenland.

There is no way that the shape of the earth, which is round, can be shown accurately on a map, which is flat. Only globes, because they are round like the earth, can show the world the way it really is. But we cannot put a globe in a book. And you would not want to carry a globe with you, to help you find your way in a foreign country. So we print flat maps.

You probably know that maps are marked off with imaginary lines. The lines of latitude run east and west. They are also called parallels because they are parallel to each other. The 0° latitude line is at the equator, midway between the earth's poles. We measure latitude in degrees north or south of the equator. The North Pole is at 90° north; the South Pole is at 90° south.

Lines of longitude, also called meridians, run north and south from the North Pole to the South Pole. There was no central line (such as the equator) to call the 0° line of longitude, so the nations of the world had to select one. In 1884, the meridian that runs through Greenwich, England, was chosen. Longitude is measured in degrees east and west of this imaginary line, which we call the Prime Meridian. In the middle of the Pacific Ocean, half-way around the world from Greenwich, is the International Date Line. When Monday morning arrives east of the Date Line, it is still Sunday night to the west of the Line.

On a globe, the meridians meet at the poles, so they get closer and closer together the farther north and south they are. On a flat map, however, meridians are often drawn parallel to each other. That is why the lands nearest the poles are stretched out and distorted.

Many of the maps you see in atlases, or on the walls

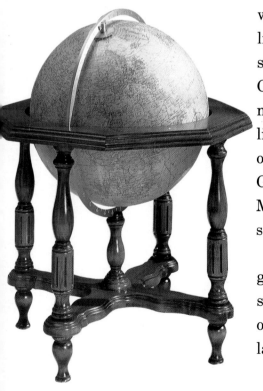

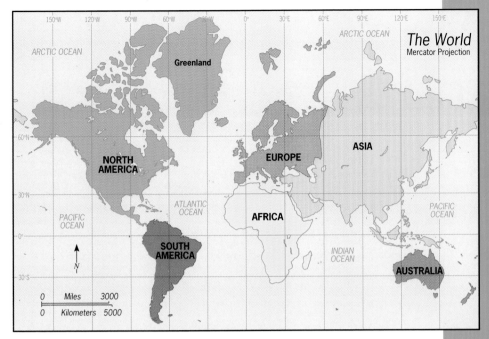

The World
Mercator Projection

On a Mercator map of the world, the lines of longitude (which meet at the Poles on a globe) are drawn parallel to each other. The Prime Meridian (0° longitude) falls in the center of the map. To make this map of the world lie flat, the North-to-South cut has been made along the International Date Line, (180° longitude). The Polar regions are not shown.

of your schoolroom, show the earth's features in this distorted way. We call these kinds of maps "Mercator projections," after Gerard Mercator. He was a Flemish mathematician and mapmaker, who, in the sixteenth century, developed this way of trying to put the round world on a flat map.

Here's a little experiment you can do to show how difficult that is:

Take an orange and draw lines of longitude on it, having them meet at the "North Pole" and the "South Pole." Tear the skin along one line of logitude and peel the orange. Try to keep the peeling all in one piece, if possible. You will find that to make it lie flat you have to make cuts in it. Like the mapmakers, you might choose to make your cuts along lines of longitude. You can see how, if you had peeled a map off a globe instead of a peeling off an orange, you would have big gaps in your map. Again, just like the mapmakers, you might choose to stretch out the land masses of the far north and the far south, just to make your map look better.

Now you know why Greenland, which is far to the north, is drawn much bigger than it really is and looks about as large as Africa.

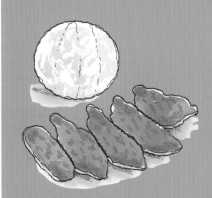

Road-Map Adventures

Planning a trip you are going to take in a car or a van is a lot of fun. To decide on the roads you will take you study road maps. The more you look at a road map, the more interesting things you see.

That is because road maps tell you about a lot more than roads.

Do you enjoy visiting historic places, like the homes of U.S. Presidents, or where a famous battle was fought? Such places are often shown on road maps. So are parks, lakes, rivers, colleges, museums, Indian reservations, National Forests, campsites, ski areas, and many other things.

Of course, the real purpose of a road map is to show you how to get from one place to another. If you are in a hurry, you can take the shortest way. But if you have the time, you might choose to go a longer, more scenic route. Scenic routes are often marked on road maps with a special line.

Road maps can guide you to where you can find a wilderness trail (top left)...to historic places like Mount Vernon, George Washington's Virginia home (top right)...and to exciting sights like Old Faithful, in Yellowstone National Park (bottom left).

14

Imagine that you live in Detroit, Michigan, and that your family is going to drive up to Bay City to spend a summer week with your grandparents. There is a direct route that will get you to Bay City in a couple of hours. Or you can go the long, scenic way, driving around Michigan's "thumb," along the shore of Lake Huron. You can still get to Bay City in a few hours if you really want to. But you might prefer to stop a few times and swim in the lake, or play on the beach. Maybe you would even like to camp overnight at one of the state parks marked on your map.

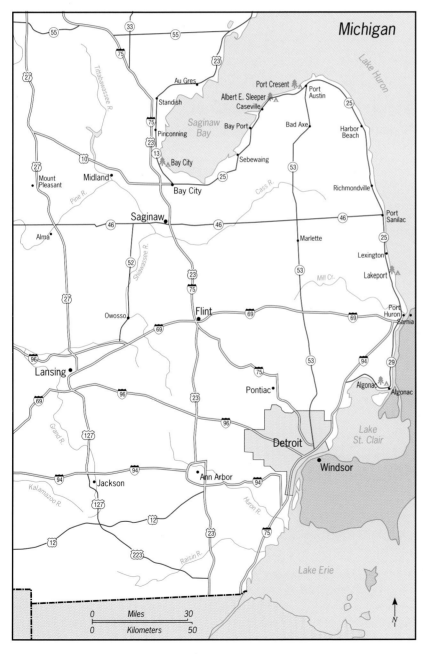

TYPICAL ROAD-MAP SYMBOLS

Road maps are available in atlases sold in bookstores. They may also be obtained from auto clubs and gas stations. Each map maker chooses different symbols and colors to represent the different types of roads and various important features. The symbols that appear below are used on maps made by the U.S. Geological Survey.

 State Parks (with camping facilities)

 State Parks (without camping facilities)

X̅ Waysides, Roadside Parks

▲ Campsite

✈ Airports

■ Points of Interest

◆ Service Area

▭ Information Center

◆ Rest Area (full facility)

◇ Rest Area (partial facility)

S.P. State Parks

S.F. State Forests

S.R. State Reserves

━━ Free Limited-Access Highways

═══ Toll Limited-Access Highways

══ Other Four-Lane Divided Highways

━━ Principal Highways

── Other Through Highways

── Other Roads

═══ Unpaved Roads

---- Scenic Routes

15

Weather Maps

There is one kind of map that changes every day, or even every hour. That's the map that shows us the weather.

Look in your daily newspaper for the weather maps. Save them for a few days and notice how they change. These maps are made by meteorologists, the people who study and predict the weather.

How do the meteorologists get all the information they need so that they can tell us what the weather is going to be like tomorrow?

Ships at sea, aircraft in the sky, balloons high up in the atmosphere, and satellites orbiting Earth carry instruments that record information about the weather. This information goes to a center in Maryland. It is drawn onto maps and sent by radio and telephone to newspapers and radio and TV stations all over the country.

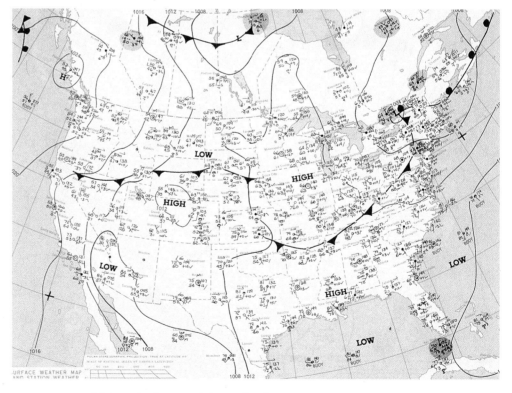

Meteorologists use information from many sources to make weather maps.

This blimp-shaped balloon will carry instruments high into the atmosphere to record information about the weather.

When your family is planning a picnic, you like to know if the weather is going to be warm or cold, sunny or rainy, windy or calm. You want to know when a storm is coming your way. If a bad storm occurs on a school day, you might even have to stay home from school!

If knowing what the weather is going to be like is important to you, think about how much more important it is to a lot of other people. Those who must keep our highways clear of snow, for instance. And airplane pilots and ships' captains. Or the farmers who grow our food and the truckers who haul it. Or the drivers of school buses. Or people who work outdoors, like builders, loggers, and fishermen. They all must know what the weather is going to be like so they can plan their work, or decide if they can even work at all. They look carefully at the weather maps in their newspapers and on TV.

Knowing what the weather is going to be like
is very important to a lot of people.

18

This map tells people living on the Southeastern coast of the United States that they should prepare for a hurricane.

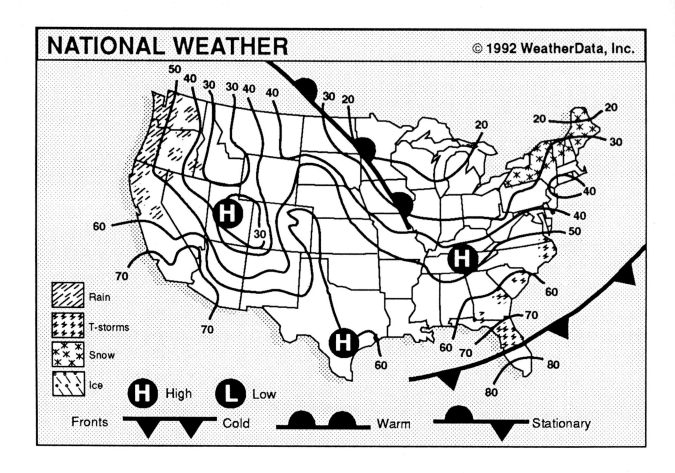

© 1992 WeatherData, Inc.

Rain
T-storms
Snow
Ice

H High **L** Low

Fronts ▼▼ Cold ●● Warm ▼ Stationary

You might like to make a scrapbook of weather maps that you clip out of your local newspaper. Some weather maps look like the one above.

On this map, areas with the same temperature are joined by a line. This map shows the weather in the United States on a day in January. It is 80° Fahrenheit (27° Celsius) in southern Florida, while in northern Minnesota temperatures are only in the 20s (about –7° Celsius). However, Minnesotans studying this map might be glad to see that there is a warm front moving in their direction.

Some newspapers print weather maps with bands of different colors running across them. Purple and blue are used for the coldest temperatures; red and orange for the warmest. The weather map to the right shows what the weather was like on a day in March.

You can see that in the south of Texas, the temperature is already summer-like, in the 80s (about 29° Celsius). In other parts of Texas, in southern

Arizona and California, and in much of the Southeast, temperatures are in the 70s (24° Celsius). But in far northern Minnesota, Michigan, and Maine, people are still shivering in 20° Fahrenheit (–7° Celsius), winter-like cold.

This map also shows that a cold front is dipping down into Texas and across Missouri, Kentucky, and North Carolina. Where cold and warm fronts meet, rain, and sometimes severe thunderstorms, develop.

An H or an L printed on the map indicates an area of high or low barometric pressure. An area of high pressure usually has calm weather. Regions around low pressure systems are likely to have rain, snow, wind, or at least cloudy skies. By studying the map's legend, you will learn what all the other symbols stand for.

If your newspaper prints weather maps in black and white, you might find it fun to color in the different bands. You could use the guide above the map that is shown in color.

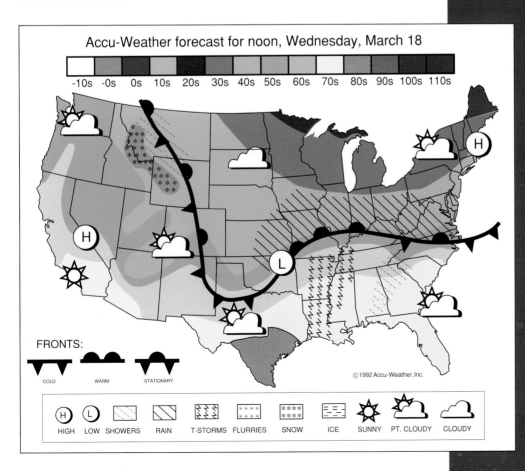

Accu-Weather forecast for noon, Wednesday, March 18

-10s -0s 0s 10s 20s 30s 40s 50s 60s 70s 80s 90s 100s 110s

© 1992 Accu-Weather, Inc.

FRONTS:

COLD   WARM   STATIONARY

(H) HIGH (L) LOW SHOWERS RAIN T-STORMS FLURRIES SNOW ICE SUNNY PT. CLOUDY CLOUDY

Mapping the Land

Have you ever seen surveyors at work? If you saw them beside a highway, they might have been helping to plan where a new shopping center or office building or gas station would be built.

If they were on a country road, they may have been checking out the boundaries of a lot where someone was going to build a house. But what if you see surveyors way out in the wilderness? What would they be doing? Most likely they would be making a map.

The oldest map we have is one carved on a piece of clay. It is about 4,000 years old. It was probably made in the same way that many maps are made today. Somebody went out and measured the land. Even the tools that surveyors use now are much like those that have been used for centuries.

Surveyors work with measuring tapes and compasses. The instrument you may have seen them looking through is called a transit. It tells them how far to the left or right something is from a certain line. Their instruments also tell them the height of a hill or mountain.

Many of the small details shown on a map are drawn with the help of a magnifying glass.

As they have done for centuries, surveyors make maps by walking the land and measuring it with instruments.

Did you know that George Washington was a surveyor and mapmaker? When he was a young soldier he drew some of the first maps ever made of the wilderness along the Ohio River. Washington drew the map that is reproduced below when he was only 14 years old. It shows his stepbrother Lawrence's turnip field.

The young country of the United States of America grew fast. More and more people moved west. The first ones into unexplored territory drew maps so that others would have an easier time finding the best ways to go. Many families in covered wagons followed maps of the Santa Fe trail or the trails that led to Oregon and California.

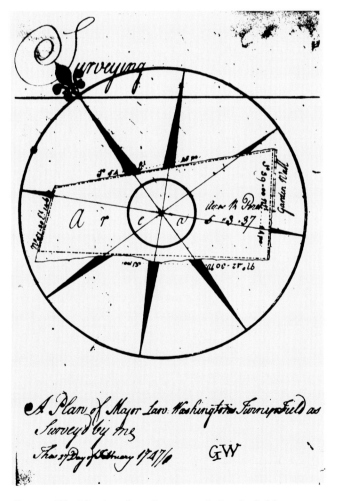

George Washington drew Lawrence's turnip field within a *compass rose* — a circle showing the points of the compass. You may have seen a small compass rose on some maps. Other maps simply use a small arrow to show you where North is.

NEW MAPS HELP SAVE OUR ENVIRONMENT

The world in which you are growing up is being made better and safer because cartographers have found a way to make maps that help protect the environment. How can maps do that? By showing what effects major changes will have on the land, the water, and other resources. These "future maps" are made on computers from images sent by satellites. Often they show the dangers of going ahead with proposed developments.

The Great Dismal Swamp National Wildlife Refuge straddles the border between North Carolina and Virginia. It is a delicately balanced ecological area that is being squeezed by both agricultural and industrial development. By using computerized satellite signals, planners saw just where such development had to be stopped if this beautiful wildlife refuge were to be saved.

In Wisconsin, a company wanted to build a new headquarters on a lake. Computer/satellite maps showed that there were places where the new buildings could not be constructed without serious damage to the lake and other nearby bodies of water.

In Arizona, a mining company wanted to trade some land it owned for land inside a National Forest. On its newly-acquired land it planned to excavate a mine. What effect would the mine have on the scenic area? Would it create an ugly scar that would spoil the natural beauty of the forest? Satellite/computer maps were programmed with data and the images were allowed to roll into the future. When the Forest Service saw the damage that would be done by the mine, they turned down the land-swap deal.

Early mapmakers often lived outdoors for months at a time. There was no way to map the wilderness except to go into it on foot or horseback. Pack trains of mules and horses carried supplies and surveying tools across hot, dry deserts and up steep, snowy mountains.

Today, many maps are made using photographs taken from directly above the region. Special cameras and viewers, carried aloft by airplanes and satellites, give mapmakers pictures in three dimensions. From these images computers can draw maps that show the exact shape of the land, its hills and valleys, its rivers and inlets. Such maps are called topographic maps.

Computers are helping cartographers make more detailed maps than we have ever had before.

Aerial and satellite photographs show changes in the shoreline and other alterations caused by nature or by people. Cartographers use these photos to correct their maps.

On a topographic map made by the U.S. Geological Survey (USGS), places at the same altitude are connected by a thin brown line. Look at the drawings above, and you will see how the land that is shown in the photograph is drawn on a map.

There is no place in the United States that hasn't been mapped. But the mapmakers are still at work. They redraw maps to show the changes made by people, such as new highways, bridges, dams, and buildings. They also have to make new maps because of earthquakes, landslides, floods, and other changes made by nature.

On topographic maps, lines and/or colors are used to convey information about the altitude of the region. Where the lines are far apart, the land is flatter. In the steeper places, the lines are closer together.

There is an extremely detailed map that shows where you live. It may even have your house and school on it. If you would like to have the map of your area, check to see if there is a map store in your city or town that sells USGS maps. If there isn't one, you can write to:

U.S. Geological Survey
Federal Center, Box 25286
Denver, CO 80225

Tell where you live. If your house is in the country, give the name of your county and the nearest town. Tell them how many miles you live from that town, and in which direction.

The USGS will write back to you, telling you how much your map will cost. It will probably be less than $3.00.

You and your friends will have a lot of fun looking at the map of the area where you live. You will find on it lots of places you know, and probably some you don't.

There is a United States Geological Survey map of the area where you live that shows your house and school.

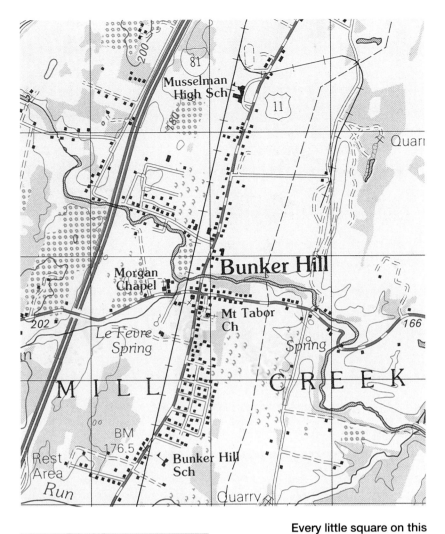

Every little square on this map indicates a house. The buildings with flags are schools.

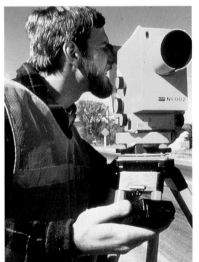

A USGS surveyor at work.

Different mapmakers may use different symbols. These are some used by the U.S. Geological Survey on its topographic maps:

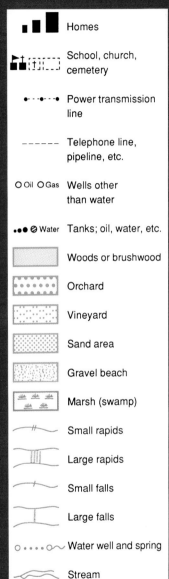

▪▪▮▮	Homes
▶†▪▪ ::::::	School, church, cemetery
•–•··•–•	Power transmission line
– – – –	Telephone line, pipeline, etc.
○ Oil ○ Gas	Wells other than water
•••● ⊘ Water	Tanks; oil, water, etc.
▭	Woods or brushwood
▦	Orchard
▦	Vineyard
▦	Sand area
▦	Gravel beach
▦	Marsh (swamp)
∿	Small rapids
∿	Large rapids
∿	Small falls
∿	Large falls
○••••○∿	Water well and spring
∿∿	Stream

Mapping the Seas

People have been mapping the world's oceans for thousands of years. Sailors of long ago traveled far from their homelands. They drew maps of the coasts and islands they explored. Their maps were not given, or even shown, to people from another country.

Ships' captains guarded their maps carefully. They didn't want them to fall into the hands of rival traders. Sometimes when an unknown craft approached a ship, the captain would weight his maps with lead and throw them overboard.

In the middle of the nineteenth century all seagoing nations decided to share their knowledge of the world's oceans. Now the seas of Earth are well mapped.

Sea maps are called charts. There are many special kinds. There are coast charts that guide ships while they are sailing in water close to shore. There are harbor charts that help ships' captains sail safely into harbors and bays. Other charts are used by a ship's captain when the ship is still offshore but close enough to land so that lights and buoys can be seen.

When a ship is far out on the open sea, with no landmarks in sight, how does the navigator know where he is? He no longer finds his position by observing the stars and the sun. Satellites now send signals that give ships their exact locations in latitude and longitude.

Ships' captains would drop their maps overboard to keep them out of the hands of rival traders.

The land under the world's oceans was once a mystery. Now we know that the land under the seas is much like the land on the continents. There are flat areas, hills, deep canyons, and even towering mountains.

In the South Pacific there is a long, deep canyon called the Marianas Trench. It is many times bigger than the Grand Canyon in Arizona.

GLOSSARY

altitude The height of a location or object above sea level.

barometric pressure. The pressure of the atmosphere as it is measured by an instrument called a barometer.

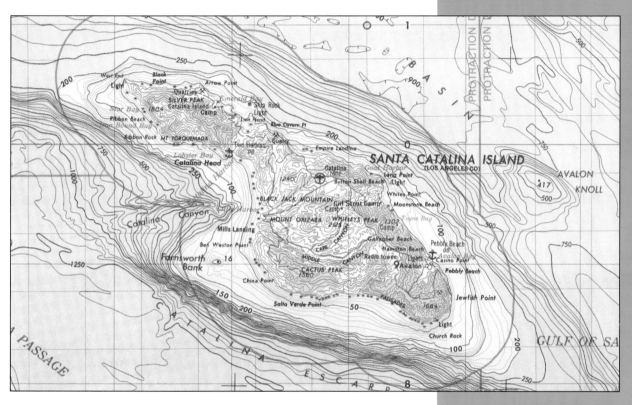

The waters around Santa Catalina Island, off California, are shown in this sea chart. The thin brown lines around the island indicate variations in the depth of the sea floor.

Divers who go deep into the oceans add details to maps of the underwater landscape.

Left: Ships at sea now determine their exact location from signals transmitted by satellites.

cartographer A person whose work is the making of maps.

compass rose A circle drawn on a map with pointers to indicate the directions of the compass.

constellation A number of stars that are thought of as a group.

equator An imaginary line around the earth that is equally distant from the North and South Poles.

floor plan A scale drawing that shows the size and layout of the rooms on one floor of a house or other building.

globe A round model of the earth that shows its different features.

29

There are huge underwater mountain chains in both the Atlantic and Pacific Oceans. Most of the peaks don't show above the water, but some do. Can you guess where the highest peaks of these mountain chains are? They rise out of the middle of the Pacific Ocean, making the beautiful islands of Hawaii.

We know about these undersea mountains and canyons because for many years we have been mapping the ocean floor. Hundreds of ships sail the seas, sending sound signals down to the bottom of the ocean. Instruments measure the time it takes for the sound to travel to the bottom of the sea and back up again. Scientists know how fast sound travels through water, so checking the time tells them the distance.

Sound waves that travel to the ocean floor and back up again
help mapmakers chart the lands beneath the sea.

Explorers of the ocean floor sometimes live in habitats such as Sealab.

Submersibles like this one take scientists down to the deepest depths of the oceans.

Many times you have heard the term *sea level*. Is the surface of the sea really level—except, of course, for waves? Scientists had always thought that it was. But an amazing fact about the oceans was discovered by a U.S. satellite. The shape of the ocean floor changes the shape of the water's surface. Scientists were able to explain why this is so. Wherever there is an underwater mountain, there is a greater pull of gravity. This pull actually draws more water to the area above the mountain. So, strange as it seems, mountains on the sea floor actually make hills in the surface of the water.

As scientists continue to investigate the mysterious lands under Earth's seas, who knows what other exciting discoveries mapmakers will be able to show on the maps of tomorrow?

latitude The distance north or south of the equator, measured in degrees.

legend On a map, the legend is the explanation of the symbols used.

longitude The distance east or west of an imaginary line that passes through Greenwich, England, and runs from the North Pole to the South Pole. Longitude is measured in degrees.

meteorologist A person trained in the science that studies the earth's atmosphere and climate.

scale In mapmaking, the word scale refers to how the size of things or places shown compares with the size of the actual things or places.

sea level The level of the surface of the sea when measured halfway between high and low tide.

surveyor A person who uses certain instruments to measure land.

symbol On a map a symbol is a mark or drawing that stands for a real object, such as a bridge, or a real feature of the landscape, such as a mountain.

topographic map An accurate and detailed map that shows the surface features of an area, such as hills, valleys, streams, lakes, marshes, roads, towns, cities, houses, etc.

transit An instrument used by surveyors for measuring horizontal angles; in other words, the degrees of angles to the right or left of a certain point. By measuring angles, surveyors are able to figure distances.

Index

Picture Credits

Brown Brothers: page 10. Gräfe und Unzer Verlag GmbH (Wil Tirion): page 5 bottom. Library of Congress: page 23. Mapping Specialist Limited, Madison, Wisconsin: pages 13 top, 15. National Center for Atmospheric Research: page 17. National Oceanographic and Atmospheric Administration: pages 16 bottom, 19, 29 bottom. Rand McNally (William Franklin McMahon): pages 24 top left, 27 bottom left. Replogle Globes, Inc.: page 12. U.S. Department of Agriculture (Ken Hammond): page 14 top left. U.S. Department of the Interior, National Park Service: page 14: bottom left. U.S. Geological Survey: pages 5 bottom right, 22, 25, 27 top, 29 top. U.S. Navy: page 31. Washington, D.C. Convention and Visitors Bureau: page 14 top right. Weather Data, Inc.: page 20. Aerial photo of Long Beach, New York courtesy of Aero Graphics Corporation, Bohemia, New York: page 24 bottom. Weather Graphics courtesy of Accu-Weather, Inc. State College, Pennsylvania: page 21.